COURT ECLOGS

COURT ECLOGS

Written in the Year, 1716

Alexander Pope's
autograph manuscript
of poems by
Lady Mary Wortley Montagu

Edited by ROBERT HALSBAND

The New York Public Library
Astor, Lenox and Tilden Foundations

&

Readex Books
A Division of Readex Microprint Corporation

THIS PUBLICATION HAS BEEN PRODUCED WITH THE ASSISTANCE OF THE ARENTS COLLECTIONS FUND.

Copyright © 1977 The New York Public Library, Astor, Lenox and Tilden Foundations; editorial matter copyright © 1977 Robert Halsband

Distributed by Readex Books

Library of Congress Cataloging in Publication Data

Montagu, Mary Pierrepont Wortley, Lady, 1689–1762.
   Court eclogs written in the year, 1716.

   Reproduced in facsim. from the ms. in the New York Public Library's Arents Tobacco Collection.

   1. Montagu, Mary Pierrepont Wortley, Lady, 1689–1762 — Manuscripts — Facsimiles. 2. Pope, Alexander, 1688–1744. II. New York. Public Library. Arents Tobacco Collection. III. Title.
PR3604.C6   1976   826'.5   76–17311
ISBN 0–87104–265–7

Contents

Introduction	vii
COURT ECLOGS, IN ALEXANDER POPE'S HAND	
Eclog I: Roxana, or the Drawingroom	3
Eclog II: St. James's Coffeehouse	11
Eclog III: The Basset Table	23
Eclog IV: The Téte-a-Téte	35
Eclog V: The Small-Pox	43
CONSTANTINOPLE, IN LADY MARY WORTLEY MONTAGU'S HAND	
Written January 1718 in the Chiosk at Pera overlooking Constantinople	53
Notes to the Introduction	63
Notes to the Text	64

INTRODUCTION

The autograph manuscript by Alexander Pope entitled by him *Court Eclogs Written in the Year, 1716* is an exceptionally interesting document. It was not he who composed these five "town eclogues," but Lady Mary Wortley Montagu.*[1] Although Lady Mary's later literary reputation is that of a versatile and accomplished letter writer she was at this time conspicuous in London court circles as the clever young wife of a staid Whig politician. Soon after Pope met her, probably in the summer of 1715, their friendship blossomed, for they had much in common. Without being a learned bluestocking Lady Mary had read widely if not deeply; and she had taught herself Latin to supplement the French and Italian lessons arranged by her father as suitable studies for an aristocratic young lady. By this time she had begun to fulfill her ambition to be a writer, although she was prevented by the decorum of her sex and social class from publishing under her name. She had written an ambitious critique of Joseph Addison's tragedy *Cato*, which was suppressed by Addison and never printed; and she had contributed an essay, anonymously, to his *Spectator* papers in 1714.[2] She now joined Pope and his friend John Gay in a literary enterprise — the composition of a set of town eclogues.

The town eclogue was a newly developed sub-genre, invented by either Gay or Swift (the honor is disputed);[3] it simply adapts Virgil's pastorals to London's beau-monde, drawing witty parallels between the rivalries and complaints of Virgil's shepherds

---

* Notes to the Introduction and to the text begin on page 63.

and shepherdesses and those of the beaux and belles of cosmopolitan polite society. Stimulated by her friendship with Pope and Gay, Lady Mary composed five eclogues, one for each weekday except Friday — for which Gay himself wrote the eclogue. Many years later she told Horace Walpole that the town eclogues "were first thought of in company with Pope and Gay. . . ."[4] Pope's share in the collaboration was evidently to suggest alterations of one kind or another; and he carefully footnoted his manuscript of the eclogues with those passages in Virgil's poems that paralleled the English adaptation.

In the fashion of the time, when squibs, lampoons, and satires — particularly if they were witty and scandalous — were circulated among friends of the writers and the victims, the eclogues were copied and the manuscripts passed about. Three of these eclogues (two by Lady Mary, the other by Gay) fell into the hands of the piratical printer Edmund Curll — his biography (by Ralph Straus) is justly entitled *The Unspeakable Curll* — who published them anonymously in March 1716 under the title *Court Poems*. This slight, scruffy pamphlet contains a teasing preface hinting that the author of the poems is either Pope or Gay or a "Lady of Quality." Pope undertook to punish Curll for his audacity in a curious way — by slyly administering an emetic and then publishing two pamphlets to describe the imagined after-effects. The full set of eclogues, meanwhile, remained unpublished.

When Lady Mary left England in August 1716 to accompany her husband on his embassy to Turkey, Pope was disconsolate (or so he lamented), but he solaced himself, he insisted, with a copy of her eclogues. In November (1716) he wrote to her that the changes at Court had very little effect on "a man who never ask'd for any thing but your Pastoralls." He proved the sincerity of his admiration when he later boasted of the "respect" he had paid her eclogues: "They lie inclosed in a Monument of Red Turkey, written in my fairest hand; the gilded Leaves are opend with no less veneration than the Pages of the Sybils; like them, lockd up & conceald from all prophane eyes: None but my own have beheld these sacred Remains of yourself, and I should think it as great a wickedness to divulge them, as to Scatter abroad the Ashes of my Ancestors."[5] What he describes here is the very manuscript — still bound in turkey-red morocco, its fore-edge gilt — whose facsimile lies before us. In giving his title page the date 1716 he must have had in mind the year he made this fair copy, for Lady Mary had composed at least several of the eclogues during the autumn of 1715.

Not long after Lady Mary returned to England (in October 1718) she was encouraged by Pope to rent a house in Twickenham. As her neighbor, with her living presence nearby, he no longer had need of her "sacred Remains." He presented to her the little album of "Court Eclogs" that he had prepared with such elegant care. Perhaps at the same time he commissioned Godfrey Kneller to paint her portrait, which he then celebrated with some poetry of his own; in these lines he praises her virtues, including those that she exhibited in her eclogues:

> Learning not vain, and wisdom not severe
> With Greatness easy, and with wit sincere.[6]

Having the album of eclogues in her possession Lady Mary evidently lent it to friends, including Lord Bathurst, who prided himself on being one of her unchangeable "humble Admirers." Pope was the intermediary for returning the precious album, writing to her (in the spring of 1720): "Lord Bathurst told me you had given orders that the book of Eclogues should be trusted to my hands to return it to you."[7] The album thus stayed in her possession. Even after her friendship with Pope had turned to bitter enmity she kept it, just as he kept his Kneller portrait of her on the wall of his best room facing the Thames.[8] When Lady Mary went abroad (in 1739) to begin an expatriation in France and Italy that lasted twenty-two years, she took the album, along with her own manuscripts and her immense library of printed books. After her death (in 1762) the Pope manuscript was inherited, together with all her possessions, by her only daughter, the Countess of Bute, and from her it descended to the Earls of Harrowby. It was acquired by George Arents in the 1940's, and is now in The New York Public Library's Arents Tobacco Collection.

Why has this manuscript found a place in a great collection devoted to the literature of tobacco? In "St James's Coffee House" (line 54) a boastful gallant tells how he has tried to snatch a snuff-box from a coy countess; in "The Bassett Table" (lines 38, 112) a lady who is making a wager uses as her forfeit a precious snuff-box given to her as a lover's pledge; and in "The Tête à Tête" (line 84) Strephon, as he attempts to seduce a reluctant young wife, takes a pinch of snuff to stimulate his eloquence. Since snuff-boxes (and their contents) were a conspicuous accessory in the beau-monde of Augustan England, it is no surprise that Lady Mary, herself a user of snuff,[9] should have furnished her eclogues with them.

While the album was in her possession Lady Mary copied into the blank pages at the back a long poem that she had composed during her residence in Constantinople. It is an intimate, subjective piece describing her thoughts and feelings as she sat in the garden of the British embassy in January 1718 looking out at the city spread below. While still in that city she had sent a copy of the poem to her uncle William Feilding, M.P, a functionary at the court of St. James's, and he proudly allowed others to admire it.[10] It thus fell into the hands of Anthony Hammond, who was compiling a collection published in May 1720 as *A New Miscellany of Original Poems, Translations and Imitations*. Exactly when Lady Mary copied the poem into her little album is uncertain — presumably before it was printed in the miscellany. If the eclogues remind us that her friendship with Pope warmed her imagination and aroused her ambition, the verses on Constantinople at the back of the album reassure us that she could by herself write brilliant verse without the assistance of the greatest poet of the age.

COURT ECLOGS

Written in the Year, 1716.

M. W. M.

TRANSCRIPT OF LADY MARY'S AUTOGRAPH [HARROWBY MS]
FACING PAGE: FACSIMILE OF POPE'S AUTOGRAPH [ARENTS MS]

Roxana
Or the Drawing-room
Monday

Roxana from the Court returning late
Sigh'd her soft sorrows at St James's Gate;
Such heavy thoughts lay brooding in her Breast
Not her own Chairmen with more weight oppress'd;
5 They groan the cruel load they're doom'd to bear,
She, in these gentler Sounds, express'd her Care.

    Was it for this, that I these Roses wear,
For this, new set my Jewells for my Hair?
Ah Princesse, with what Zeal have I persu'd!
10 Almost forgot [the] Dutys of a Prude,
Thinking I never could attend too soon,
I've miss'd my Prayers to get dress'd by noon.

ECLOG . I.

ROXANA, or the Drawingroom.

^x ROXANA *from the Court returning late,*
Sigh'd her soft Sorrows at St. James's Gate.
Such heavy thoughts lay brooding in her breast,
Not her own Chairmen with more weight opprest:
They groan'd the cruel Load they're doom'd to bear;
She in these gentler Sounds exprest her care.

Was it for this that I these Roses wear,
For this, new-sett the Jewels for my Hair?
Ah Princess! with what zeal have I pursu'd?
Almost forgot the Duties of a Prude!
Thinking I never could attend too soon,
I've miss'd my Pray'rs, to get ~~me~~ *dress'd by Noon.*

^x Formosum pastor Corydon &c. Virg. Ecl. 2.

For

FROM HARROWBY MS

    For thee, Ah what for Thee did I resign!
    My Pleasures, Passions, all that e're was mine.
15 I sacrificed both modesty and ease,
    Left Operas, and run to filthy Plays;
    Double Entendres shock'd my tender Ear,
    Yet even this for thee I chose to bear.
    In glowing Youth when Nature bids, be Gay,
20 And ev'ry Joy of Life before me lay,
    By Honor prompted, and by Pride restrain'd,
    The Pleasures of the Young my Soul disdain'd,
    Sermons I sought, and with a mein severe
    Censured my Neighbours, and said daily Pray'r.
25 Alas how chang'd! With the same sermon meen
    That once I pray'd, the What d'ee callt I've seen.
    Ah cruel Princesse! for thy sake I've lost
    That Reputation which so dear had cost.
    I, who avoided every Public place
30 When Bloom, and Beauty bid me shew my Face,
    Now near thee constant ev'ry Night abide
    With never failing Duty by thy side:
    My selfe and Daughters standing on a row
    To all the foreigners a goodly Show!

For thee, ah what for thee did I resign?
My Pleasures, Passions, all that e'er was mine.
I sacrific'd both Modesty, and Ease,
Left Opera's, and run to filthy Plays.
Double-Entendres shock'd my tender ear,
And yet all these, for thee, I chose to bear.
In glowing Youth, when Nature bids be gay,
And ev'ry Joy of Life before me lay;
By Honour prompted, and by Pride restrain'd,
The Pleasures of the Young my Soul disdain'd.
Sermons I sought, and with a Mien severe,
Censur'd my Neighbors, and said Daily Pray'r.
Alas! how chang'd? with the same Sermon-mien
That once I pray'd, the * What-dyecall't I've seen.
Ah royal Princess! for thy sake I lost
That Reputation, which so dear had cost.
I who avoided ev'ry publick place,
When Bloom and Beauty bid me show my face,
Now, near thee constant ev'ry night abide,
With never-failing Duty by thy side:
Myself and Daughters standing in a Row,
To all the Foreigners a Goodly Show!

* The name of a Farce, which some Prudes
scrupled to go to, on the score of the Title.   Oft

FROM HARROWBY MS

35 Oft had your drawing room been sadly thin
And Merchants' Wives close by the Chair had been,
Had not I amply fill'd the empty Space
And sav'd your Highness from the dire Disgrace.
Yet Coquettilla's Artifice prevails
40 When all my Merit and my Duty fails,
That Coquettilla, whose deluding airs
Corrupts our Virgins, and our Youth ensnares:
So sunk her Character, so lost her Fame,
Scarce visited before your Highness came,
45 Yet for the Bed chamber, 'tis her you chuse,
When Zeal, and fame, and virtue you refuse.
Ah worthy Choice! not one of all your Train
Whom Censure blasts not, or Dishonors stain.
Let the Nice Hind now suckle dirty Pigs
50 And the Proud Peahen hatch the Cuckow's Eggs,
Let Iris leave her Paint, and own her Age,
And Grave Suffolkia wed a giddy Page,
A great[er] Miracle is daily veiw'd,
A vertuous Princesse with a Court so lewd.
55 I know thee, Court! with all thy treacherous wiles,
Thy false Carreses and undoing smiles!

Oft had your Drawing-Room been sadly thin,
And Merchants Wives close by your Chair had been,
Had I not Amply fill'd the empty Space,
And sav'd Your Highness from the dire Disgrace.
Yet Coquetilla's Artifice prevails,
When all my Duty and my Merit fails.
That Coquetilla, whose deluding Airs
Corrupts our Virgins, and our Youth ensnares:
So sunk her Character, so lost her Fame,
Scarce Visited, before your Highness came!
Yet for the Bed-chamber 'tis She you chuse,
While Zeal, and Fame, and Virtue, you refuse.
‡ Ah worthy Choice! not one of all your Train
Whom Censure blasts not, or Dishonours stain.
† Let the nice Hind now suckle dirty Pigs,
And the proud Pea-hen hatch the Cuckow's Eggs;
Let Iris leave her Paint, and own her Age,
And grave Su— cia wed a Giddy Page;
A greater Miracle is daily view'd,
A virtuous Princess with a Court so lewd.
× I know thee, Court! and all thy treach'rous wiles,
Thy false Caresses, and undoing Smiles!

‡ O digno conjuncta viro! &c. Virg. Ecl. 8.   Ah...
† Jungentur jam gryphes equis—&c. Virg. Ec. 8. Nunc & ovis ultro fugiat lupus &c.
× Nunc scio quid sit Amor — Ibid.

FROM HARROWBY MS

    Ah Princesse! learn'd in all the courtly Arts,
    To cheat our Hopes, and yet to gain our Hearts!

        Large lovely Bribes are the great Statesman's Aim
60   And the neglected Patriot follows Fame,
    The Prince is *ogle'd*, some the King persue,
    But your Roxana only follows you.

        Despis'd Roxana, cease, and try to find
    Some other, since the Princesse proves unkind,
65   Perhaps it is not hard to find at Court
    Thô not a greater, a more firm support.

Ah Princess! learn'd in all the Courtly Arts,
To cheat our Hopes, and yet to gain our Hearts!
  × Large, lovely Bribes are the great Statesman's [Aim,
And the neglected Patriot follows Fame;
The Prince is ogled; some the King pursue;
But your Roxana only follows You.
† Despis'd Roxana cease, and try to find
Another, since your Princess proves unkind.
Perhaps it is not hard to gain at Court
If not a greater, a more firm Support.

  × Torva laena lupum sequitur, &c. Te Corydon, o Alexi — Virg.
  † O Corydon, quæ te dementia cepit, Invenies alium, si hic te fastidit, Alexin. Ibid.

ECL-

Tuesday

St James's Coffee-house

Silliander and Patch

Thou who so many Favours hast receiv'd,
Wondrous to tell and hard to be beleiv'd,
Oh H——d, to my Lays Attention lend,
Hear how two Lovers boastingly contend,
5   Like thee successfull, such their bloomy Youth,
Renown'd alike for Gallantry and Truth.

    St James's bell had toll'd some wretches in,
As tatter'd Riding hoods alone could sin,
The happier Sinners now their Charms recruit
10   And to their Manteaus their Complexions suit.

ECLOG II.

St. James's Coffeehouse.

THOU, who so many Favors hast receiv'd,
Wondrous to tell, and hard to be believ'd,
Oh H—d! to my ~~lowly~~ Lays attention lend,
Hear how two Lovers boastingly contend:
Like thee successful, such their bloomy Youth,
Renown'd alike for Gallantry, and Truth.

St. James's Bell had toll'd some Wretches in;
As tatter'd Riding-hoods alone could sin:
The happier Sinners now their charms recruit,
2 And to their Manteaus their Complexions suit.
Nice Ladies loath with such a Crowd to mix,
1 For none but ragged Matrons pray at Six.

The

FROM HARROWBY MS

   The Opera Queens had finish'd halfe their Faces
And City Dames allready taken Places,
Fops of all kinds to see the Lion run,
The Beauties wait till the first Act's begun
15 And Beaux step home to put fresh Linnen on.
No well dress'd Youth in Coffee house remain'd,
But pensive Patch, who on the Window lean'd,
And Silliander, that Alert and gay,
First pick'd his Teeth and then began to say.

Silliander

20 Why all these sighs, ah why so pensive grown?
Some cause there is that thus you sit alone.
Does hopeless Passion all this Sorrow move?
Or dost thou Envy, where the Ladies love?

Patch

If whom they love, my envy must persue,
25 'Tis sure at least I never envy you.

Silliander

No, I'm unhappy, you are in the right,
'Tis you they favour, and tis me they slight.
Yet I could tell—but that I hate to boast—
A Club of Ladies, where 'tis me they toast.

The Opera-Queens had finish'd half their faces,
And City Dames already taken Places:
Fops of all kinds to see the *Lion run,
The Beauties wait till the First Act's begun,
And Beaus step home to put fresh Linnen on.
No well-drest Youth in Coffeehouse remain'd,
But pensive Patch, who on the window lean'd;
And Silliander, that <u>alert</u> and gay,
First pick'd his Teeth, and then began to say.

Silliander.

Why all these Sighs? ah why so thoughtful grown?
Some cause there is that thus you sit alone.
Does hopeless Passion all this Sorrow move,
Or dost thou envy where the Ladies love?

Patch.

If whom they love my Envy must pursue,
'Tis sure at least I never envy You.

Silliander.

No, I'm unhappy, you are in the right,
'Tis you they favour, and 'tis me they slight.
Yet I could tell — but that I hate to boast —
A Club of Ladies, where 'tis me they toast.

    * A famous Scene in the Opera of Hydaspes,   Patch.
where Nicolini kills a Lyon.

FROM HARROWBY MS

Patch

30   Toasting does seldom any favour prove,
Like us they never toast the Thing they love.
A certain Duke one night my health begun,
With cheerfull Pledges round the Room it run,
Till the young Silvia, press'd to drink it too,
35   Started, and vow'd she knew not what to do:
What, drink a fellow's health! she dy'd with Shame,
Yet blush'd when ever she pronounced my Name.

Silliander

Ill fate persue me, may I never find
The dice propitious or the Ladys kind
40   If fair Miss Flippy's fan I did not tear,
And one from me she condescends to wear.

Patch

Women are allways ready to receive,
'Tis then a favour when the Sex will give.
A Lady (but she is too great to name,
45   Beauteous in Person, spotless in her Fame)
With gentle Strugglings let me force this Ring,
Another Day may give Another Thing.

Patch.

Toasting does seldom any favour prove;
Like us, they never toast the thing they love.
A certain Duke one night my Health begun,
With chearful Pledges round the Room it run,
Till the young Sylvia, prest to drink it too,
Started, and vow'd she knew not what to do:
What, drink a Fellow's health? She dy'd wth shame;
Yet blush'd whenever she pronounc'd my name.

Silliander.

Ill Fate pursue me! may I never find
The Dice propitious, or the Ladies kind,
Or what's yet worse to each well-judging Spark,
My Wigg be ruffled when I walk the Park!
If fair Miss Hippy's Fan I did not tear,
And one from me she condescends to wear.

Patch.

Women are always ready to receive;
Tis then a Favour when the Sex will give.
A Lady (but she is too great to name)
Beauteous in Person, spotless in her Fame,
With gentle Struglings let me force this Ring;
† Another Day may give another Thing.

† Aurea mala decem misi, Cras altera mittam.

Sil-

FROM HARROWBY MS

Silliander

    I could say something — see this Billet doux —
    And as for presents — look upon my shooe —
50 These Buckles were not forc'd, and halfe a Theft,
    But a young Countess fondly made the Gift.

Patch

    My Countess is more nice, more artfull too,
    Affects to fly, that I may fierce persue.
    This Snuff box, while I begg'd, she still deny'd,
55 And when I strove to snatch it, seem'd to hide,
    She laugh'd, and fled, and as I sought to seize
    With Affectation cramm'd it down her Stays:
    Yet hoped she did not place it there unseen;
    I press'd her Breasts, and pull'd it from between.

Silliander

60 Last Night as I stood ogling of her Grace,
    Drinking Delicious Poison from her Face,
    The soft Enchantress did that face decline
    Nor ever rais'd her Eyes to meet with mine,
    With sudden art some secret did pretend,
65 Lean'd cross two chairs to whisper to a Freind,
    While the stiff whalebone with the motion rose
    And thousand Beauties to my sight expose.

Silliander.

I could say something — see this Billet-doux!
And as for Presents, look upon my Shooe —
These Buckles were not forc'd, or half a Theft,
But a young Countess fondly made the Gift.

Patch.

My Countess is more nice, more artful too;
*Affects to fly, that I may fierce pursue:
This Snuffbox, while I begg'd she still deny'd,
And when I strove to snatch it, seem'd to hide;
She laugh'd and fled; and as I sought to seize,
With Affectation cramm'd it down her Stays:
Yet hop'd she did not place it there unseen;
I press'd her Breasts, and pull'd it from between.

Silliander.

Last night as I stood ogling of her Grace,
Drinking delicious Poyson from her Face;
The soft Enchantress did that Face decline,
Nor ever rais'd her eyes to meet with mine:
With careless art some Secret did pretend,
Lean'd cross two Chairs to whisper to a Friend;
While the stiff Whalebone with the Motion rose,
And thousand Beauties to my eyes expose.

* *malo me Galatea petit — Et fugit ad salices, sed se cupit ante videri.* Virg. Ecl. 3. *At mihi sese offert, &c.* Ibid.   Patch

FROM HARROWBY MS

Patch

      Early this morn (but I was ask'd to come)
      I drunk Bohea in Cælia's dressing room,
70   Warm from her Bed, to me alone within,
      Her Nightgown fasten'd with a single Pin,
      Her Nightcloaths tumble'd with resistless Grace
      And her bright Hair play'd careless round her Face.
      Reaching the Kettle, made her Gown unpin,
75   She wore no Wastcoat, and her Shift was thin.

Silliander

      See Titiana driving to the Park,
      Hast, let us follow, 'tis not yet too Dark
      In her all Beauties of the Spring are seen,
      Her Cheeks are rosy, and her mantua Green.

Patch

80   See Tintoretta to the Opera goes,
      Hast, or the Croud will not permit our Bows,
      In her the Glory of the Heavens we view,
      Her Eyes are star-like, and her mantua blue.

Silliander

      What Colour does in Cælia's stockings shine?
85   Reveal that secret and the Prize is thine.

Patch

      What are her Garters? tell me if you can,
      I'll freely own thee for the happy man.

Patch.
Early this morn (but I was ask'd to come)
I drank Bohea in Cælia's Dressing-room:
Warm from her Bed, to me alone within,
Her Nightgown fasten'd with a single Pin.
Her Headcloths tumbled with resistless grace,
And her bright Hair play'd careless round her face:
Reaching the Kettle made her Gown unpin,
She wore no Wastcote, and her Shift was thin.

Silliander.
See Titiana driving to the Park;
Hast, let us follow, 'tis not yet too dark.
In her all Beauties of the Spring are seen,
Her Cheeks are rosie, and her Manteau green.

Patch.
See Tintoretta to the Opera goes;
Hast, or the Crowd will scarce permit our Bows.
In her the Glories of the Heav'ns we view,
Her Eyes are Star-like, and her Manteau blew.

Silliander.
*What Colour does in Celia's Stockings shine?
Reveal that Secret, and the Palm is thine.

Patch.
What are her Garters, tell me if you can,
I'll freely own thee for the happy Man.

*Dic quibus in terris &c. Ibid.

Thus

FROM HARROWBY MS

    Thus Patch continu'd his Heroic Strain
While Silliander but contends in vain.
90   After a Conquest so important gain'd
    Unrivall'd Patch in ev'ry Ruelle reign'd.

ˣ Thus Patch continu'd his Heroic Strain,
While Silliander but contends in vain.
After a Conquest so important gain'd,
Unrival'd Patch in ev'ry Ruelle reign'd.

ˣ Hæc memini, et victum frustra contendere Thyrsin,
Ex illo Corydon, Corydon est tempore nobis. Virg. Ec. 7.

Thursday

The Bassette Table

Smilinda, Cardelia

Cardelia

The Bassette Table spread, the Tallier come,
Why stays Smilinda in the dressing room?
Rise, pensive Nymph! The Tallier stays for you —

Smilinda

Ah Madam! since my Sharper is untrue,
5   I joyless make my once ador'd Alpieu.
I saw him stand behind Ombrelia's Chair,
And whisper with that soft deluding Air
And those feign'd sighs that cheat the list'ning Fair.

Cardelia

Is this the cause of your Romantic Strains?
10 A mightier greife my heavy Heart sustains;
As you by Love, so I by Fortune crost,
In one bad deal three sept le va's I lost.

ECLOG III.

The Basset Table.

Cardelia.

THE Basset Table spread, the Tallier come,
Why stays Smilinda in the Dressing-room?
Rise pensive nymph! the Tallier waits for you.

Smilinda.

Ah Madam! since my Sharper is untrue,
I joyless make my once-ador'd Alpue.
I saw him stand behind Ombrelia's chair,
And whisper with that soft deluding Air
And those feign'd sighs that cheat the listning Fair.

Cardelia.

Is this the cause of your romantic Strains?
A mightier grief my heavy Heart sustains:
As you by Love, so I by Fortune crost,
In one bad Deal, three Septleva's have lost.

Smi-

FROM HARROWBY MS

Smilinda

Is that a Greife that you compare with mine?
With ease the Smiles of Fortune I resign,
15   Would all my Gold in one bad Deal were gone
Were lovely Sharper mine, and mine alone.

Cardelia

A Lover lost is but a common Care
And prudent Nymphs against the Change prepare.
The Queen of Clubs thrice lost! Oh, who could guess
20   This fatal stroke, this unforeseen distress?

Smilinda

See Betty Loveit, very a propos!
She all the pains of Love and Play does know,
Deeply experience'd many years ago.
Dear Betty shall th'Important point decide,
25   Betty, who oft the pains of each has try'd;
Impartial she shall say who suffers most,
By Cards' ill usage, or by Lovers lost.

Loveit

Tell, tell your Greife, attentive will I stay,
Tho' Time is precious, and I want some Tea.

Cardelia

30   Behold this Equipage by Mathers wrought,
With fifty Guineas (a great pen'north) bought.

Smilinda.

Is that the grief which you compare with mine?
With ease the Smiles of Fortune I resign:
Would all my Gold in one bad Deal were gone,
Were lovely Sharper mine, and mine alone.

Cardelia.

A Lover lost is but a common care,
And prudent Nymphs against the Change prepare.
The Queen of Clubs thrice lost! oh who could guess
This fatal Stroke, this unforeseen distress!

Smilinda

See Betty Love-it, very a-propos!
She all the cares of Love and Play does know,
Deeply experienc'd many years ago.
Dear Betty shall th' important Point decide,
Betty, who oft the pain of each has try'd;
Impartial She shall say, who suffers most,
By Cards ill usage, or by Lovers lost.

Loveit.

Tell, tell your griefs; attentive will I stay,
Tho' Time is precious, and I want some Tea.

Cardelia.

†Behold this Equipage, by Mathers wrought,
With fifty Guineas (a great Penn'worth) bought.

†—pocula ponam Fagina, cælatum divini opus Alcimedontis, &c. See

FROM HARROWBY MS

    See, on the Tooth pick Mars and Cupid strive,
    And both the struggling Figures seem alive.
    Upon the bottom, see the Queen's bright Face,
35 A Myrtle Foliage round the Thimble Case.
    Jove, Jove himselfe does on the Scissars shine;
    The Metal, and the Workmanship Divine!

Smilinda

    This Snuff box once the Pledge of Sharper's love
    When Rival Beauties for the present strove,
40 (At Corticelli's he the Raffle won,
    There first his Passion was in Public shown,
    Hazardia blush'd, and turn'd her Head aside,
    A Rival's envy, all in vain, to hide)
    This Snuff box — on the hinge see Brillants shine!
45 This Snuff box will I stake, the Prize is mine.

Cardelia

    Alas! far lesser Losses than I bear,
    Have made a Soldier sigh, a Lover swear.
    But oh what makes the Disapointment hard,
    'Twas my own Lord, who drew the Fatal Card!
50 In complaisance I took the Queen he gave,
    Thô my own secret Wish was for the Knave:
    The Knave won Sonica that I had chose
    And the next pull, my sept le va I lose.

See on the Toothpick, Mars and Cupid strive,
And both the strugling Figures seem alive.
Upon the bottome, Loe! the Queen's bright Face;
A Myrtle Foliage round the Thimble-case.
Jove, Jove himself does on the Scizzars shine;
The Metal, and the Workmanship, divine!
    Smilinda.
This Snuff-box, once the pledge of Sharpers love,
When rival Beauties for the present strove.
(At Corticelli's he the Raffle won,
Then first his Passion was in publick shown;
Hazardia blush'd, and turn'd her head aside,
A Rival's envy, all in vain, to hide.)
This Snuff-box — on the hinge see Brilliants shine!
This Snuff-box will I stake, the Prize is mine.
    Cardelia.
Alas! far lesser losses than I bear,
Have made a Soldier sigh, a Lover swear.
And oh! what makes the disappointment hard,
'Twas my own Lord that drew the fatal Card!
In complaisance, I took the Queen he gave,
Tho' my own secret wish was for the Knave:
The Knave won Sonica, which I had chose;
And the next Pull, my Septleva I lose.

    Smilinda

FROM HARROWBY MS

Smilinda

But ah, what agravates the killing smart,
55 The cruel thought that stabs me to the Heart:
This curst Ombrelia, this undoing Fair,
By whose vile arts this heavy Greife I bear,
She, at whose Name, I shed these spitefull Tears,
She owes to me the very Charms she wears.
60 An aukard Thing when first she came to Town,
Her Shape unfashion'd, and her Face unknown,
She was my Freind; I taught her first to spread
Upon her sallow cheeks enlivening Red.
I introduce'd her to the Parks and Plays,
65 And by my Interest Cosins made her Stays.
Ungratefull Wretch! with Mimic airs grown pert,
She dares to steal my Fav'rite Lover's Heart.

Cardelia

Wretch that I was! how often have I swore
When Winnall tally'd, I would punt no more?
70 I know the Bite, yet to my ruin run,
And see the Folly which I cannot shun.

Smilinda

How many Maids have Sharper's vows deceiv'd?
How many curs'd the moment they beleiv'd?
Yet his known Falsehood could no warning prove,
75 Ah what are Warnings to a Maid in Love!

Smilinda.

But ah! what aggravates the killing Smart,
The cruel thought that stabs me to the heart:
This curs'd Ombrelia, this undoing Fair,
By whose vile arts this heavy grief I bear
She, at whose name I shed these spiteful Tears,
She owes to me the very charms she wears.
An awkward Thing, when first she came to Town,
Her Shape unfashion'd, and her Face unknown;
She was my Friend; I taught her first to spread
Upon her sallow cheeks enlivening Red.
I introduced her to the Parks and Plays,
And by my Int'rest, Cozens made her Stays.
Ungrateful Wretch! with Mimic Airs grown pert,
She dares to steal my Fav'rite Lovers heart.

Cardelia.

Wretch that I was! how often have I swore
When Winnall tally'd, I would punt no more?
I know the Bite, yet to my ruin run,
And see the Folly which I cannot shun.

Smilinda.

How many Maids have Sharper's Vows deceiv'd?
How many curs'd the moment they believ'd?
Yet his known falshoods could no Warning prove,
Ah what is Warning to a Maid in love?

Cardelia

FROM HARROWBY MS

Cardelia

But of what Marble must that Breast be form'd,
Can gaze on Bassette and remain unwarm'd?
When Kings, Queens, Knaves, are set in decent Rank,
Expos'd in Glorious heaps, the tempting Bank!
80 Guineas, halfe guineas, all the shineing Train,
The Winner's Pleasure, and the Loser's pain;
In bright Confusion open Rouleaus lie,
They strike the Soul, and glitter in the Eye:
Fir'd by the sight, all Reason I disdain,
85 My passions rise, and will not bear the Rein.
Look upon Bassette, you who reason boast,
And see if Reason may not there be lost!

Smilinda

What more than Marble must the Breast compose
That listens coldly to my Sharper's vows?
90 Then, when he trembles, when his Blushes rise,
When Awfull Love seems melting [in] his Eyes!
With eager Beats, his Mechlin Cravat moves:
He loves! I whisper to my selfe, He loves!
Such unfeign'd Passion in his Looks appears,
95 I lose all mem'ry of my former Fears;
My panting Heart confesses all his Charms,
I yeild at once, and sink into his Arms.
Think of that Moment, you who Prudence boast;
For such a Moment, Prudence well were lost!

Cardelia.

But of what Marble must that breast be form'd,
To gaze on Basset, and remain unwarm'd?
When Kings, Queens, Knaves, are set in decent rank;
Expos'd in glorious heaps the tempting Bank!
Guineas, Half-guineas, all the shining Train;
The Winners Pleasure and the Loser's Pain:
In bright confusion open Ruleaus lie,
That strike the Soul, and glitter in the Eye:
Fir'd by the sight, all reason I disdain;
My Passions rise, and will not bear the Rein.
Look upon Basset, you who reason boast,
And see if reason may not there be lost!

Smilinda.

What more than Marble must that heart compose,
That listens coldly to my Sharpers vows?
Then, when he trembles! when his blushes rise!
When awful Love seems melting in his eyes!
With eager Beats his Mechlin Cravat moves:
He loves! I whisper to myself, he loves!
Such unfeign'd Passion in his looks appears,
I lose all mem'ry of my former fears;
My panting heart confesses all his charms,
I yield at once, and sink into his Arms.
Think of that moment, You who Prudence boast;
For such a moment, Prudence well were lost!

Cardelia

FROM HARROWBY MS

Cardelia

100 At the Groom Porter's, batter'd Bullys play;
Some Dukes at Marrow bone bowl Time away.
But who the Bowl or rattling Dice compares
To Bassette's heavenly Joys, and pleasing Cares?

Smilinda

Soft Semplicetta doats upon a Beau,
105 Prudina likes a Man, and laughs at Shew.
Their several graces in my Sharper meet,
Strong as the Footman, as the Master sweet.

Loveit

Cease your Contention, which has been too long,
I grow Impatient, and the Tea too strong,
110 Attend and Yeild to what I now Decide,
The Equipage shall grace Smilinda's side,
The Snuff Box to Cardelia I decree:
So, leave Complaining, and begin your Tea.

Cardelia.

* At the Groom-Porter's, batter'd Bullies play;
Some Dukes at Marybone bowl Time away.
But who the Bowl or rattling Dice compares,
To Basset's heav'nly joys, and pleasing cares?

Smilinda.

Soft Simplicetta doats upon a Beau;
Prudina likes a Man, and laughs at Show:
Their several Graces in my Sharper meet,
Strong as the Footman, as the Master sweet.

Love-it.

Cease your contention, which has been too long;
I grow impatient, and the Tea too strong.
Attend, and yield to what I now decide;
The Equipage shall grace Smilinda's Side,
The Snuff-box to Cardelia I decree:
Now leave complaining, and begin your Tea.

x Dulce satis humor, &c. mihi solus Amyntas. Virg. Ecl. 3.
Populus Alcidæ gratissima &c. Fraxinus in sylvis &c. Ecl. 7.

Wednesday
The Tête à Tête
Dancinda

No; fair Dancinda no; You strive in vain,
To calm my Care, and mitigate my Pain,
If all my sighs, my tears can fail to move,
Ah, sooth me not with fruitless vows of Love. —

5   Thus Strephon spoke, Dancinda thus reply'd:
What must I do to gratify your Pride?
Too well you know (ungratefull as thou art)
How much you triumph in this tender Heart.
What proofe of Love remains for me to grant?
10 Yet still you teize me with some new Complaint!
Oh, would to Heaven (but the fond wish is vain)
Too many favours had not made it plain!
But such a passion breaks through all disguise,
Love reddens on my Cheek, and wishes in my Eyes.

15   Is't not enough, Inhuman and unkind!
I own the secret conflict of my Mind?

ECLOG IV.

The *Téte-a-Téte*.

No fair Dancinda, no — you strive in vain
To calm my cares, or mitigate my pain!
If all my sighs, my tears can fail to move,
Ah sooth me not with fruitless vows of Love —
Thus Strephon spoke, Dancinda thus reply'd:
What must I do to gratify your Pride?
Too well you know (ungrateful as thou art)
How much you triumph in this tender heart.
What proof of Love remains for me to grant?
Yet still you teize me with some new complaint?
Oh would to Heav'n! (but the fond wish is vain)
Too many favors had not made it plain!
But such a Passion breaks thro' all disguise,
Love reddens on my cheek, & wishes in my Eyes.
 Is't not enough, Inhuman and unkind!
I own the secret conflict of my mind?

You

FROM HARROWBY MS

You cannot know what torturing Pain I prove,
When I with burning Blushes own, I love.
You see my artless Joy at your Approach,
20 I sigh, I faint, I tremble at your touch,
And in your Absence, all the World I shun,
I hate Mankind, and curse the cheering Sun;
Still as I fly, ten thousand Swains persue;
Ten thousand Swains I sacrifice to you:
25 I shew you all my Heart, without Disguise:
But these are tender proofes that you despise —
I see too well what Wishes you persue;
You would not only Conquer, but undo.
You, Cruel Victor, weary of your Flame,
30 Would seek a Cure in my Eternal Shame;
And not content my Honor to subdue,
Now strive to triumph o're my Virtu too.

Oh Love! A God indeed to Womankind!
(Whose Arrows burn me, and whose fetters bind)
35 Avenge thy Altars, vindicate thy fame,
And blast these Traitors who prophane thy Name,
Who by pretending to thy sacred Fire,
Raise Cursed Trophys to impure Desire!

Have you forgot, with what ensnaring Art
You first seduce'd this fond, uncautious Heart?

You cannot know what tort'ring pain I prove,
When I with burning blushes own, I Love.
You see my artless joy at your approach;
I sigh, I faint, I tremble at your touch;
And in your absence all the world I shun;
I hate the day, and curse the chearing Sun:
Still as I fly, a thousand Swains pursue;
A thousand Swains I sacrifice for you:
I show you all my thoughts without disguise:
But these are tender proofs that you despise.—
I see too well what wishes you pursue;
You would not only conquer, but undoe.
You cruel Victor, weary of your flame,
Would seek a cure in my eternal Shame;
And not content my Honour to subdue,
Now strive to triumph o'er my Virtue too.

Oh Love! a God indeed to Womankind!
(Whose Arrows burn me, and whose Fetters bind)
Avenge thy Altars, vindicate thy fame,
And blast the Traytors who prophane thy name;
Who, by pretending to thy sacred fire,
Raise guilty Trophies to impure Desire!

Have you forgot, with what ensnaring art
You first seduc'd a fond, uncautious heart?

Then

FROM HARROWBY MS

    Then as I fled, did you not, kneeling, cry,
    Turn, Cruel Beauty! whither would you fly?
    Why all these doubts, why this distrustfull Fear?
    No impious Wishes shall offend your Ear,
45 Nor ever shall my boldest Hopes pretend
    Above the Title of a tender Freind.
    Blest if my Lovely Goddess will permit
    My humble vow, thus sighing at her feet!
    The Tyrant Love that in my Bosom reigns,
50 The God himselfe submits to wear your chains,
    You shall direct his Course, his Ardour tame,
    And check the Fury of his wildest Flame.

      Unpractis'd Youth is easily deceiv'd,
    Sooth'd by such sounds, I listen'd, and beleiv'd:
55 Now quite forgot that soft submissive Fear,
    You dare to ask, what I must blush to hear.

      Could I forget the Honor of my Race,
    And meet your wishes, fearless of Disgrace;
    Could Passion o're my tender Youth prevail,
60 And all my Mother's pious Maxims fail:
    Yet to preserve your Heart (which still must be,
    False as it is, for ever dear to me)
    This fatal proofe of Love, I would not give,
    Which you contemn the moment you receive.
65 The wretched she who yeilds to guilty Joys,
    A Man may pity, but he must despise.

      Your Ardour ceas'd, I then should see you shun
    The wretched victim by your Arts undone,

Then, as I fled, did you not kneeling cry,
Turn, cruel Beauty! whither would you fly?
Why all these doubts, ~~and~~ why this distrustful fear?
No impious wishes shall offend your ear:
Nor ever shall my boldest hopes pretend,
Beyond the title of a tender Friend.
Blest, if my lovely Goddess shall permit
My humble vows, thus sighing at her feet!
The Tyrant Love that in my bosom reigns,
The God himself, submits to wear your chains;
You shall direct his course, his ardour tame,
And check the fury of his wildest flame.

    Unpractis'd youth is easily deceiv'd;
Sooth'd by such words, I listen'd and believ'd:
Now quite forgot that soft submissive fear,
You dare to ask what I must blush to hear.

    Could I forget the honour of my Race,
And meet your wishes, fearless of Disgrace;
Could Passion o'er my tender youth prevail,
And all my Mother's pious maxims fail:
Yet, to preserve your heart, (which still must be
False as it is, for ever dear to me)
This fatal proof of Love I would not give,
Which you contemn the moment you receive,
2 { Your ardour ceas'd, I then should see you shun
   The hapless Victim by your arts undone.
1 { ye wretched she, who yields to guilty Joys Yet
   A Man may pity, but he must despise.

FROM HARROWBY MS

    Yet if I could that cold Indifference bear,
70 What more would strike me with the last Despair,
    With this Refflection would my Soul be torn,
    To know I merited your cruel Scorn.

        Has Love no pleasures free from Guilt or Fear?
    Pleasures less feirce, more lasting, more sincere?
75 Thus let us gently kiss, and fondly Gaze,
    Love is a Child, and like a Child he plays.

        Oh Strephon! if you would continu Just,
    If Love be something more than Brutal Lust;
    Forbear to ask, what I must still deny,
80 This bitter Pleasure, this Destructive Joy;
    So closely follow'd by the Dismal Train
    Of cutting Shame, and Guilt's heart peirceing Pain.

        She paus'd; and fix'd her Eyes upon her Fan,
    He took a pinch of snuff, and thus began,
85 Madam, if Love — but he could say no more
    For Made'moiselle came rapping to the Door.

        The dangerous Moments no Adieus afford,
    Begone, she crys, I'm sure I hear my Lord.
    The Lover starts from his unfinish'd Loves,
90 To snatch his Hat, and seek his scatter'd Gloves,
    The sighing Dame to meet her Dear prepares;
    While Strephon cursing slips down the back Stairs.

Yet if I could your cold Indifference bear,
What more would strike me with the last despair
With this Reflection would my Soul be torn,
To know, I merited your cruel Scorn!

Has Love no pleasures free from guilt & fear?
Pleasures less fierce, more lasting, & sincere?
Thus let us gently kiss, and fondly gaze;
Love is a Child, and like a Child he plays.

O Strephon! if you would continue just,
If Love be something more than brutal Lust;
Forbear to ask what I must still deny,
This bitter pleasure, this destructive joy;
So closely follow'd by the wretched Train
Of cutting Shame, & Guilt's heart-piercing Pain.

She paus'd, then fixt her eyes upon her Fan:
He took a Pinch of Snuff, and thus began.
Madam, if Love — But he could add no more,
For Mademoiselle came rapping at the door.
The dang'rous moments no adieus afford;
Begone, she cries, I'm sure I hear my Lord —
The Lover starts from his unfinish'd Loves
~~the~~
To snatch his Hat, & seek his scatter'd Gloves
The sighing Dame to meet her Dear prepares
While Strephon cursing slips down y͏ᵉ Back stairs

Satturday

The Small Pox

Flavia

The wretched Flavia, on her Couch reclin'd,
Thus breath'd the Anguish of a wounded mind.
A Glass revers'd in her right hand she bore;
For now she shunn'd the Face she sought before.

5   How am I chang'd! Alas, how am I grown
A frightfull Spectre to my selfe unknown!
Where's my Complexion, where the radiant bloom
That promis'd Happyness for Years to come?
Then, with what Pleasure I this Face survey'd!
10 To look once more, my Visits oft delay'd!
Charm'd with the veiw, a fresher red would rise,
And a new Life shot sparkling from my Eyes.
Ah Faithless Glass, my wonted bloom restore!
Alas, I rave! that bloom is now no more!

ECLOG V.

The Small-Pox.

THE wretched Flavia, on her Couch reclin'd,
Thus breath'd the anguish of a wounded mind.
A Glass revers'd in her right hand she bore;
For now she shunn'd the Face she sought before.

How am I chang'd! alas, how am I grown
A frightful Spectre to my self unknown!
Where's my Complexion, where that radiant Bloom
Which promis'd happiness for years to come?
Then with what pleasure I this Face survey'd?
To look once more, my Visits oft delay'd.
Charm'd by the view, a fresher Red would rise,
And a new Life shot sparkling from my eyes!
Ah faithless Glass! my wonted Bloom restore:
I rave in vain — that Bloom is now no more!

The

FROM HARROWBY MS

15 The Greatest Good the Gods on Men bestow,
Even Youth it selfe to me is useless now.
There was a Time, (Oh that I could forget!)
When Opera Tickets pour'd before my Feet,
And at the Ring where brightest Beauties shine,
20 The earliest Cherrys of the Park were mine.
Wittness oh Lilly! and thou Motteux tell!
How much Japan these Eyes have made you sell,
With what contempt you saw me oft despise
The humble Offer of the raffle'd Prize:
25 For at each raffle still the Prize I bore,
With Scorn rejected, or with Triumph wore:
Now Beautie's Fled, and Presents are no more.

  For me, the Patriot has the House forsook,
And left debates to catch a passing look,
30 For me, the Soldier has soft verses writ,
For me, the Beau has aim'd to be a Wit,
For me, the Wit to Nonsense was betraid,
The Gamester has for me his Dun delaid,
And overseen the Card, I would have paid.
35 The bold and Haughty, by Success made vain,
Aw'd by my Eyes has tremble'd to complain,
The bashfull 'Squire touch'd with a wish unknown
Has dar'd to speak with Spirit not his own,

The greatest Good the Gods on Man bestow,
Ev'n Youth itself, to me is useless now.
There was a time (oh that I could forget!)
When Opera-Tickets pour'd before my feet,
And at the Ring where brightest Beauties shine,
The earliest Cherries of the Park were mine.
Witness oh Lilly! and thou Motteux tell!
How much Japan these Eyes have made you sell.
With what contempt you saw me oft despise
The humble Offer of the raffled Prize:
For at each Raffle still the Prize I bore,
With scorn rejected, or with triumph wore:
Now Beauty's fled, and Presents are no more!

For me, the Patriot has the House forsook,
And left Debates to catch a passing Look:
For me the Soldier has soft Verses writ:
For me the Beau has aim'd to be a Wit:
For me the Wit to Nonsence was betray'd:
~~For me~~ the Gamester has, for me, his Dun delay'd,
And over-seen the Card I would have ~~paid~~:
The bold and haughty, by Success made vain,
And by my eyes, have trembled to complain:
The bashful Squire, touch'd with a wish unknown,
Has dar'd to speak, with Spirit not his own.

Fir'd

Fir'd by one Wish, all did alike Adore,
Now Beauty's fled, and Lovers are no more.

    As round the Room I turn my weeping Eyes,
New unaffected Scenes of Sorrow rise;
Far from my Sight that killing Picture bear,
The Face disfigure, or the Canvas tear!
That Picture, which with Pride I us'd to show,
The lost ressemblance but upbraids me now.
And thou my Toilette! where I oft have sate,
While Hours unheeded pass'd in deep Debate,
How Curls should fall, or where a Patch to place,
If Blue or Scarlet best became my Face;
Now on some happier Nymph thy Aid bestow,
On Fairer Heads, ye useless Jewells, glow!
No borrow'd Lustre can my Charms restore,
Beauty is fled, and Dress is now no more.

    Ye meaner Beauties, I permit you, shine,
Go triumph in the Hearts, that once were mine,
But midst your Triumphs, with Confusion know,
'Tis to my Ruin all your Charms ye owe.
Would pitying Heaven restore my wonted mein,
You still might move, unthought of, and unseen —
But oh, how vain, how wretched is the boast,
Of Beauty faded, and of Empire lost!
What now is left, but weeping to Deplore
My Beauty fled, and Empire now no more!

Fir'd by one Love, all did alike adore;
Now Beauty's fled, and Lovers are no more!

   As round the room I turn my weeping eyes,
New, unaffected Scenes of Sorrow rise.
Far from my sight that killing Picture bear,
The ~~lines~~ dis-figure, or the canvas tear!
That Picture which with pride I us'd to show,
The lost Resemblance ~~but~~ upbraids ~~affects~~ me now.
And thou, my Toilette! where I oft have sate,
While Hours unheeded past in deep debate,
How Curls should fall, and where the Patch to place,
If Blue or Scarlet best became my face;
Now on some happier nymph thy aid bestow;
On fairer heads, ye useless Jewels, glow!
No borrow'd Lustre can my charms restore:
Beauty is fled, and Dress is now no more!

   Ye meaner Beauties! I permit you, shine,
Go triumph in the hearts that once were mine!
Yet 'midst your triumphs, with confusion know,
Tis to my Ruin all your charms ye owe.
Would pitying Heav'n restore my former mien,
You still might move, unthought of, and unseen—
But oh! how vain, how wretched is the boast,
Of Beauty faded, and of Empire lost?
What now is left, but weeping to deplore
My Beauty fled, and Empire now no more!

                                         Ye

FROM HARROWBY MS

65   Ye cruel Chymists, what withheld your Aid?
        Could no Pomatums save a trembling Maid?
        How false and triffling is that Art you boast;
        No Art can give me back my Beauty lost!
        In tears surrounded by my Freinds I lay,
70   Mask'd o're, and trembling at the light of Day,
        Mirmillo came my Fortune to deplore
        (A golden headed Cane, well carv'd he bore),
        Cordials, he cry'd, my Spirits must restore,—
        Beauty is fled, and Spirit is no more!
75   Galen the Grave, Officious Squirt was there,
        With fruitless Greife and unavailing Care;
        Machaon too, the Great Machaon, known
        By his red Cloak, and his superior frown,
        And why (he cry'd) this Greife, and this Dispair?
80   You shall again be well, again be fair,
        Beleive my Oath (with that an Oath he swore),
        False was his Oath! my Beauty is no more.

           Cease hapless Maid, no more thy Tale persue,
        Forsake Mankind, and bid the World Adieu.
85   Monarchs, and Beauties rule with equal sway,
        All strive to serve, and Glory to obey,
        Alike unpity'd when depos'd they grow,
        Men mock the Idol of their Former vow.

Ye cruel Chymists! what with-held your aid?
Could no Pomatums save a trembling Maid?
How false and trifling is the art you boast;
No art can give me back my Beauty lost!
In Tears, surrounded by my Friends I lay,
Mask'd o'er, and trembling at the light of Day;
* Mirmillo came, my fortune to deplore,
(A golden-headed Cane, well-carv'd, he bore)
Cordials, he cry'd, my Spirits must restore —
Beauty is fled, and Spirits are no more!

Galen the grave, officious Squirt was there,
With fruitless grief, and unavailing care.
Machaon too; the fam'd Machaon, known
By his red Cloak, and his superior frown:
And why (he cry'd) this Sorrow and despair?
You shall again be well, again be fair;
Believe my Oath, (with that an Oath he swore)
False was his Oath! my Beauty is no more!

Cease hapless maid! no more thy Tale pursue,
Forsake mankind, and bid the world adieu.
Monarchs and Beauties rule with equal sway;
All strive to serve, and glory to obey;
Alike unpity'd, when depos'd, they grow;
Men mock the Idol of their former vow.

* Venit et upilio — Omnes, unde amor iste, rogant, tibi! venit Apollo —
Venit et agresti capitis Sylvanus honore — Pan deus Arcadiæ venit,
quem vidimus ipsi Sanguineis ebuli baccis, minioque rubentem. Adieu
                                                    Virg. Ec. 10.

FROM HARROWBY MS

      Adieu ye Parks, in some obscure recess,
90 Where Gentle streams will weep at my Distress,
Where no false Freind will in my Greife take part,
And mourn my Ruin with a Joyfull Heart,
There let me live, in some deserted Place,
There hide in shades this lost Inglorious Face.
95 Ye Operas, Circles, I no more must view!
My Toilette, Patches, all the Wo⟨rl⟩d Adieu!

Adieu ye Parks! In some obscure recess,
Where gentle Streams will weep at my distress,
Where no false Friend will in my grief take part,
Or mourn my ruin with a joyful heart;
There let me live, in some deserted place;
There hide in Shades this lost, inglorious Face.
Ye Opéras, Circles I no more must view!
My Toilett, Patches, all the World, adieu!

F I N I S.

TRANSCRIPT OF LADY MARY'S AUTOGRAPH [HARROWBY MS]
FACING PAGE: FACSIMILE OF LADY MARY'S AUTOGRAPH [ARENTS MS]

Constantinople

To ——

Give me, Great God (said I) a Little Farm
In Summer shady and in Winter warm,
Where a clear Spring gives birth to a cool brook
By nature sliding down a Mossy rock,
5   Not artfully in Leaden Pipes convey'd
Nor greatly falling in a forc'd Cascade,
Pure and unsulli'd winding through the Shade.
All-Bounteous Heaven has added to my Prayer
A softer Climat and a Purer air.

10   Our frozen Isle now chiling winter binds,
Deform'd with rains and rough with blasting winds,
The wither'd woods grown white with hoary froast
By driving Storms their verdent Beauty's lost,
The trembling Birds their leafless coverts shun
15 And seek in Distant Climes a warmer Sun,
The water Nimphs their Silenc'd urns deplore,
Even Thames benum'd, a river now no more;
The barren meadows give no more delight,
By Glistening Snow made painfull to the Sight.

Written ~~at Constantinople~~
January 1718
in the Chiosk at Pera
overlooking Constantinople

Give me Great God (said I) a little Farm
in Summer shady, & in Winter warm
where a cool spring gives birth to a cheer'd brook
by Nature slideing down a mossy Rock
Not artfully in Leaden Pipes convey'd
Or greatly falling in a forc'd Cascade
Pure & unsully'd winding throu yͤ Shade.
All bounteous Heaven has added to my Praier
a softer Climate and a purer Air.

Our Frozen Isle now chilling Winter binds
Deform'd by Rains, & rough wͤᵗ blasting Winds
yͤ wither'd Woods grown white wͤ hoary Frost
by Driving storms their scatter'd beautys lost
The Trembling birds their leaveless coverts shun
And seek in distant Climes a warmer Sun
The Water Nymphs their silenc'd Urns deplore
Even Thames benumb'd a River now no more
The barren Meadows give no more delight
by glist'ning Snows made painfull to yͤ sight

FROM HARROWBY MS

20   Here Summer reigns with one Eternal Smile,
And Double Harvests bless the happy Soil.
Fair, fertile, fields! to whom indulgent Heaven
Has every charm of every Season given,
No killing Cold deforms the beauteous year,
25 The Springing flowers no comeing winter fear,
But as the Parent rose decayes and dyes
The infant buds with brighter collours rise
And with fresh Sweets the Mother's-Scent Supplies.
Near them the Vi'let glows with odours blest
30 And blooms in more than Tyrian Purple drest,
The rich Jonquills their golden gleem display
And shine in glory emulating day.
These chearfull groves their Living Leaves retain,
The streams still murmur undefil'd by rain,
35 And rising green adorns the fruitfull plain.
The warbling Kind uninterrupted Sing,
Warm'd with enjoyment of perpetual Spring.

    Here from my Window I at once survey
The crouded City, and Resounding Sea,
40 In Distant views see Asian Mountains rise
And lose their Snowy Summits in the Skies.
Above those Mountains high Olympus tow'rs
(The Parliamental seat of heavenly Pow'rs).

Here Summer reigns wth one eternal Smile
And double Harvests bless ye happy Soil.
Fair, fertile Fields to wm Indulgent Heaven
Has every charm of every season given!
No killing Cold deforms ye Beauteous year
The springing Flowers no coming Winter fear
But as ye Parent Rose decays & dies
ye Infant Buds wth brighter Colours rise
And with fresh sweets ye Mother-scent supplys
Near ym the Vi'let glows wth odours blest
And blooms in more than Tyrian Purple drest
The rich Jonquils their golden gleam display
And shine in glorys emulateing Day.
These chearfull Groves their living Leaves retain
The Streams still murmur undefil'd by Rain
And growing Green adorns ye fruitfull Plain
The warbling Kind uninterrupted sing,
Warm'd wth Enjoyment of perpetual Spring.

Here from my Window I at once survey
The crouded City, & resounding Sea
In distant Views see Assian Mountains rise
And Lose their Snowy Summits in ye Skies
Above those Mountains high Olympus Tow'rs
The Parliamental seat of Heavenly Powers.

FROM HARROWBY MS

      New to the sight, my ravish'd Eyes admire
45   Each gilded Crescent and each antique Spire,
      The Marble Mosques beneath whose ample Domes
      Fierce Warlike Sultans sleep in peacefull Tombs.
      Those lofty Structures, once the Christian boast,
      Their Names, their Glorys, and their Beautys lost,
50   Those Altars bright with Gold, with Sculpture grac'd,
      By Barbarous Zeal of Savage Foes defac'd:
      Sophia alone her Ancient Sound retains
      Thô unbeleiving Vows her shrine prophanes.
      Where Holy Saints have dy'd, in Sacred Cells
55   Where Monarchs pray'd, the Frantic Derviche dwells.
      How art thou falln, Imperial City, low!
      Where are thy Hopes of Roman Glory now?
      Where are thy Palaces by Prelates rais'd;
      Where preistly Pomp in Purple Lustre blaz'd?
60   Where Grecian Artists all their Skill display'd
      Before the Happy Sciences decay'd,
      So vast, that youthfull Kings might there reside,
      So splendid, to content a Patriarch's pride,
      Convents where Emperours profess'd of Old,
65   The Labour'd Pillars that their Triumphs told

New to yᵉ sight my ravish'd Eyes admire
Each guilded Crescent & each Antique Spire
~~The Marble Mosques beneath whose Ample Domes~~
~~Fierce Warlike Sultans sleep in peacefull~~
The Fair Serail where sunk in Idle ease
The Lazy Monarch melts his thoughtless Days
The Marble Mosques beneath whose Ample Domes
Fierce Warlike Sultans sleep in peacefull Tombs
Those lofty Structures once the Christian boast
Their Names, their Honours, & their Beautys lost
Those Altars bright wᵗʰ Gold, wᵗʰ sculpture grac'd
By barbarous Zeal of savage Foes defac'd
Convents where Emperors profess'd of Old
The Labour'd Pillars that their Triumphs told.
Vain Monuments of Men that once were great!
Sunk, undistinguish'd, by one Common Fate!
How art thou falln Imperial City, Low!
Where are thy Hopes of Roman Glory now?
Where are thy Palaces by Prelates rais'd
Where preistly Pomp in Purple Lustre blaz'd
So vast, that youthfull Kings might there reside
So Splendid; to content a Patriarchs pride
Where Grecian Artists all their skill display'd
Before yᵉ happy Sciences decay'd;
So vast, that youthfull Kings might there reside
So splendid, to content a Patriarchs Pride.
Convents where Emperors profess'd of Old,
The Labour'd Pillars that their Triumphs told,

(Vain Monuments of Men that once were great!)
Sunk undistinguish'd in one common Fate!

  One Little Spot the small Fenar contains,
Of Greek Nobillity, the poor remains,
70 Where other Helens show like powerfull Charms
As once engag'd the Warring World in Arms,
Those Names which Royal Auncestry can boast
In mean Mechanic arts obscurely lost,
Those Eyes a second Homer might inspire,
75 Fix'd at the loom, destroy their useless Fire.

  Greiv'd at a view which strikes upon my Mind
The short-liv'd Vanity of Humankind,
In Gaudy Objects I indulge my Sight
And turn where Eastern Pomp gives Gay Delight.
80 See the vast Train in Various Habits drest,
By the bright Scimetar and sable vest,
The Vizier proud, distinguish'd o're the rest.
Six slaves in gay Attire his Bridle hold,
His Bridle rich with Gems, his stirrups Gold,
85 His snowy Steed adorn'd with Lavish Pride,
Whole troops of Soldiers mounted by his Side,
These toss the Plumy Crest, Arabian Coursers guide.
With awfull Duty, all decline their Eyes,
No Bellowing Shouts of noisie crouds arise,
90 Silence, in solemn state the March attends
Till at the Dread Divan the slow Procession ends.

Vain Monuments of Men that once were great!
Sunk, undistinguish'd in one common Fate.

One little Spot, the small Pezar contains,
Of Greek Nobillity, the poor Remains;
Where other Helens show like powerfull Charms
As once engag'd the Warring World in Arms:
Those Names that Roial auncestry can boast
In mean Mechanic Arts obscurely lost
Those Eyes a second Homer might inspire,
Fix'd at the Loom, destroy their useless Fire.

Greiv'd at a view wch strikes upon my Mind
The short liv'd Vanity of Human kind
In Gaudy Objects I indulge my Sight,
And turn where Eastern Pomp gives gay Delight.

See, the vast Train in various Habits dress'd!
By the Bright Scymetar and Sable Vest,
The Vizier proud, distinguish'd o're the rest!
Six Slaves in gay Attire his Bridle hold;
His Bridle rough with Gemms, his Stirups Gold;
His Snowy Steed adorn'd with lavish Pride
Whole Troops of Soldiers mounted by his Side
These toss the Plumy Crest, Arabian Coursers guide)
With awfull Duty all decline their Eyes,
No bellowing Shouts of noisy Crouds arise;
Silence in solemn State the march attends
Till at the dread Divan the slow procession ends.

Yet not these prospects, all profusely Gay,
The gilded Navy that adorns the Sea,
The rising City in Confusion fair,
95 Magnificently form'd irregular,
Where Woods and Palaces at once surprise,
Gardens, on Gardens, Domes on Domes arise,
And endless Beauties tire the wandring Eyes,
So sooths my wishes or so charms my Mind
100 As this retreat, secure from Human kind,
No Knave's successfull craft does Spleen excite,
No Coxcomb's Tawdry Splendour shocks my Sight,
No Mob Alarm awakes my Female Fears,
No unrewarded Merit asks my Tears,
105 Nor Praise my Mind, nor Envy hurts my Ear,
Even Fame it selfe can hardly reach me here,
Impertinence with all her tattling train,
Fair sounding Flattery's delicious bane,
Censorious Folly, noisy Party rage,
110 The thousand Tongues with which she must engage
Who dare have Virtue in a vicious Age.

Yet not these Objects all profusely Gay,
The Gilded Navy that adorns the sea;
The riseing City in confusion fair;
Magnificently form'd irregular
Where Woods and Palaces at once surprize
Gardens, on Gardens, Domes on Domes arise
And endless Beauties tire the wandering Eyes;
So sooths my Wishes, or so charms my Mind,
As this Retreat, secure from Humankind.
No Knaves successfull Craft does Spleen excite
No Coxcombs tawdry Splendor shocks my Sight,
No Mob Alarm awakes my Female Fears,
No unrewarded Merit asks my Tears;
Nor Praise my Mind, nor Envy hurts my Ear,
Even Fame it selfe can hardly reach me here,
Impertinence with all her Talking Train
Fair-sounding Flatterys delicious Bane
Censorious Folly; Noisy Party Rage;
The Thousand with which she must engage,
Who dare have Virtue in a Vicious age.

Notes to the Introduction

In all these Notes, LM stands for Lady Mary Wortley Montagu.

1 For further material on the eclogues, see Robert Halsband "Pope, Lady Mary, and the *Court Poems* (1716)" *PMLA* 68 (1953) 237–50, and *The Life of Lady Mary Wortley Montagu* (1956) 48–55. The definitive text of the eclogues is printed in LM *Essays and Poems* ed R. Halsband and I. Grundy (1977) 182–204.

2 The critique is printed in full in LM *Essays and Poems* 62–68; the *Spectator* paper is No. 573.

3 "A Town Eclogue," printed in the *Tatler* continuation (1711), is generally regarded as one of the earliest examples; it has been attributed to Jonathan Swift but rejected by his editor (*Poems* ed H. Williams [1937] III 1087–89); and Gay's "Araminta," published in a 1714 miscellany as "A Town Eclogue" (though he later labeled it "An Elegy"), is clearly an early specimen (*Poetry and Prose* ed V. A. Dearing and C. E. Beckwith [1974] I 83–86, II 508–10).

4 Walpole *Correspondence* ed W. S. Lewis et al. (1937–   ) XIV 242.

5 Pope *Correspondence* ed G. Sherburn (1956) I 370, 441.

6 Pope *Minor Poems* ed N. Ault and J. Butt (1954) 212.

7 Pope *Correspondence* III 134, II 39.

8 *Notes and Queries* 6th Ser. V (1882) 364.

9 When she went abroad (in 1739) French customs officers at Calais confiscated from her two pounds of snuff (*Complete Letters* ed R. Halsband [1965–67] II 141).

10 *Complete Letters* III 169.

Notes to the Text

Pope's autograph is so legible that no transcript is printed here. Instead, the printed text facing the facsimile is that of the most authoritative version of LM's town eclogues, her own fair copy, contained in a notebook that she endorsed: "all the verses and Prose in this Book were wrote by me, without the assistance of one Line from any other. Mary Wortley Montagu" (Harrowby MSS, vol 256, owned by the Earl of Harrowby, now at Sandon Hall, Stafford; and printed here with the kind permission of Lord Harrowby). In 1740, when she met Horace Walpole in Florence, LM allowed him to copy out the eclogues, and she identified for him "all the persons alluded to" (Walpole *Correspondence* XIV 38, n. 40). His identifications, given in the notes below, are taken from his copy of the printed eclogues (now owned by W. S. Lewis), for which he provided Dodsley with the text: *Six Town Eclogues; With some other Poems. By the Rt. Hon. L. M. W. M.* (1747).

Page 1: LM signed her initials on the title page.

Page 2, title, Roxana: Mary Ker (1677–1718), Duchess of Roxburghe, a prude by reputation. The Drawing Room was the reception held at Court on several evenings a week during the season.

Page 2, line 9, Princesse: Caroline of Anspach (1683–1737), consort of the Prince of Wales, later George II.

Page 2, line 12: LM deleted "me" in Pope's MS. It was restored by Walpole for the 1747 edition, and in fact is required for the meter.

Page 3, Latin footnote: "Corydon, the shepherd, [was aflame for] the fair [Alexis], etc." (Virgil, ii. 1). The translations from Virgil's eclogues are adapted from the Loeb Classical Library edition (1938), ed H. R. Fairclough.

Page 4, line 24: According to Lady Cowper, the Duchess "does not care what she says of Anybody to wreak her Malice or Revenge" (Mary, Countess Cowper *Diary* ed S. Cowper 2nd ed [1865] p 78).

Page 4, line 26: *The What D'ye Call It*, a farce by John Gay, was staged at Drury-Lane in Feb 1715. Its very title is sexually suggestive, as Pope's footnote implies. The Prince and Princess of Wales had, in fact, seen it (Pope *Correspondence* I 282–83).

Page 4, line 34, foreigners: Many in George I's entourage were Hanoverians; and Coquettilla, Roxana's rival, was an Italian (married since 1705 to an English duke).

Page 6, line 39, Coquettilla: Adelaide Paleotti (d. 1726), Duchess of Shrewsbury, had been appointed Lady of the Bedchamber to the Princess of Wales in Oct 1714. At Court she "had a wonderful Art at entertaining and divert-

ing People, though she would sometimes exceed the Bounds of Decency....
she was the most cunning, designing Woman alive" (Mary, Countess Cowper
Diary 8–9).

Page 6, line 52, Suffolkia: There were two elderly Lady Suffolks, widows of
the 3rd and 5th Earls; "wed a giddy": substituted by LM for "marry with
her."

Page 7, first Latin footnote: "O wedded to a worthy lord! etc." (Virgil, viii. 32).
Charles Talbot (1660–1718), 1st Duke of Shrewsbury, had held high government posts since the reign of William and Mary; he was at this time
Groom of the Stole and Keeper of the Privy Purse to George I.

Page 7, second Latin footnote: "Griffins now shall mate with mares, etc."
(Virgil, viii. 27). "Now let the wolf even flee before the sheep, etc." (Virgil,
viii. 52).

Page 7, third Latin footnote: "Now know I what Love is" (Virgil, viii. 43).

Page 9, first Latin footnote: "The grim lioness follows the wolf, etc." / "Corydon [follows] you, O Alexis" (Virgil, ii. 63, 65).

Page 9, second Latin footnote: "O Corydon, what madness has gripped you [?]
You will find another Alexis, if this one scorns you" (Virgil, ii. 69, 73).

Page 10, title: St James's Coffee-House, according to *The Tatler* No. 1, was a
center for foreign and domestic news. Silliander, identified by Walpole as
"General J. Campbell," was probably John Campbell (ca 1693–1770), later
4th Duke of Argyll; and Patch: Algernon Seymour (1684–1750), Earl of
Hertford and (1748) 10th Duke of Somerset.

Page 10, line 3: Walpole filled in the name "Howard," probably meaning
Charles Howard (d. 1765), younger son of the 3rd Earl of Carlisle. Pope
had written "lowly" before "Lays" but then crossed it out.

Page 11, last two lines: This couplet is omitted in LM's fair copy.

Page 13, footnote: *Idaspe fedele* was a popular opera by Francesco Mancini,
first staged in 1710, when LM saw it (*Complete Letters* I 22). The castrato
Nicolino (Nicolò Grimaldi) was generally ridiculed for this scene, for example in the *Spectator* No. 13.

Page 14, line 40: Although Pope clearly wrote Hippy, LM almost as clearly
wrote Flippy, and Horace Walpole read it as that, as the 1747 printed edition
shows.

Page 15, Latin footnote: "I have sent ten golden apples, tomorrow I shall send
a second ten" (Virgil, iii. 71).

Page 16, line 61: In "Eloisa to Abelard" (1717) Pope used the same image in "Still drink delicious poison from thy eye" (line 122); and in her copy of that poem LM annotated the line with the word "mine" (Halsband *Life of LM* 76).

Page 17, Latin footnote: "Galatea pelts me with an apple, [saucy girl,] and she runs off to the willows, and hopes to be seen first."/"But [Amyntas] comes to me [unsought], etc." (Virgil, iii. 64–66).

Page 19, Latin footnote: "Tell me in what lands, etc." (Virgil, iii. 104).

Page 21, Latin footnote: "This I remember, and how Thyrsis, vanquished, strove in vain. From that time it is Corydon, Corydon with us" (Virgil, vii. 69–70).

Page 22, title: Smilinda was LM herself, and Cardelia, Elizabeth Hervey (1676–1741), Countess of Bristol, whose passion for cards was well known. LM (in 1722) refers to her "Occupations of Hazard and Bassette" (*Complete Letters* II 17). The progress of the card game, as detailed in the eclogue, is copied here from Dr Grundy's annotations, with her kind permission.

In her own fair copy of the eclogues LM places this one as IV, and the following one as III.

Page 22, Line 1, Tallier: "The *Talliere* is he that keeps the Bank." He frequently made a large profit ([Charles Cotton] *The Compleat Gamester ... to which is added, the Game at Basset* [1709] 178, 184).

Page 22, line 4, Sharper: John Dalrymple (1673–1747), 2nd Earl of Stair. Elsewhere Walpole credits Stair with being LM's lover before her marriage (*Correspondence* XIV 243).

Page 22, line 5, Alpieu: decision to raise to stake after an initial win, signalled "by turning up, or crooking the corner of the winning Card" (*Compleat Gamester* 180).

Page 22, line 6, Ombrelia: "Mrs Hanbury," probably Bridget (d. 1741), wife of John Hanbury, M. P., and mother of Sir Charles Hanbury Williams.

Page 22, line 12: sept-et-le-va is a successful "second Chance" which pays seven times the stake (*Compleat Gamester* 180).

Page 23: the authorship of this eclogue was assigned to Pope by Curll, whose credibility is nil, and by Bishop Warburton, who in the 1751 edition of Pope's works printed it "from a copy corrected by his own hand" (VI 56). Pope told Joseph Spence (in Dec 1743) that he had "a blotted copy of L^y M^{ys} Eclogues, somewhere by him" (loose papers, Osborn Collection, Beinecke Library, Yale University); this may have been the source of Warburton's error.

Page 24, line 19, Queen: substituted in Pope's MS by LM for "Knave."

Page 24, line 21, Betty Loveit: "Mrs Southwell," probably Elizabeth, a friend of Lady Bristol's, and daughter of Sir Robert Southwell (John Hervey *Letter-Books* [1894] II 153).

Page 24, line 30: Equipage is "a little case which held a thimble, scissors, a pencil, and other such little matters, and . . . hung to the girdle" (*OED*). Charles Mather, the toyman, had "brought toys in fashion, and baubles to perfection. He is admirably well versed in screws, springs, and hinges, and deeply read in knives, combs or scissors, buttons or buckles" (*The Tatler*, No. 142).

Page 24, line 31, pen'north: a bargain.

Page 25, Latin footnote: "I will stake two beechen cups, the embossed work of divine Alcimedon etc." (Virgil, iii. 36–37).

Page 26, line 40, Corticelli's: an Italian warehouse on Suffolk Street, much frequented by people of fashion for raffles, purchases, and gallant meetings.

Page 26, line 52, Sonica: card having an immediate effect on the game (*OED*).

Page 28, line 67, Lover's: substituted by LM for "Sharper's."

Page 30, line 82, Rouleaus: "a number of gold coins made up into a cylindrical packet" (*OED*).

Page 30, line 87, may: substituted by LM for "must."

Page 30, line 92, Mechlin Cravat: a neckerchief made of lace from Mechlin (in Belgium).

Page 32, line 101, Some Dukes: John Sheffield (1648–1721), Duke of Buckingham, went regularly to Marylebone, "a Place of air and exercise" (Sheffield *Works* [1723] II 278). It contained bowling-greens.

Page 33, Latin footnote: "Sweet to the corn is a shower, etc. [and] to me Amyntas alone" (Virgil, iii. 82–83). "The poplar is most dear to Alcides, etc. [Fairest is] the ash in the woods, etc." (Virgil, vii. 61, 65).

Page 36, lines 29–30: the first words of these lines, altered by LM, were originally "O" and "You."

Page 38, line 43: the second part of the line, altered by LM, probably read "and why this dismal fear?"

Page 38, line 48, humble vow: substituted by LM for "humblest vows."

Page 39: The couplet at the bottom of the page was inserted by LM.

[67]

Page 40, line 71, Soul: substituted by LM for "breast."

Page 40, line 87, Adieus: substituted by LM for "replies."

Page 40, line 89, Loves: substituted by LM for "joys" to rhyme with "gloves" newly inserted in line 90.

Page 40, lines 90–92: LM's new conclusion, written in her own hand.

Page 41: three lines near the bottom of the page, struck out by LM, can be almost completely restored:
> The Lady <?falters> with a Look, and cries
> Ah thoughtless Youth! what moments have you mist?
> You have but listen'd when you should have kist.

Page 42, title: Walpole identifies Flavia as LM, who had contracted smallpox in Dec 1715. According to her granddaughter, LM "always said she meant Flavia . . . for herself" while recovering from the illness (Lady Louisa Stuart "Biographical Anecdotes" in LM *Essays and Poems* 35).

Page 44, line 19, the Ring: a circular driveway in Hyde Park, where the beaumonde displayed themselves in coaches.

Page 44, line 21: Charles Lillie, a perfumer and seller of snuff, had been a distributor of the *Tatler* and the *Spectator*. Peter Anthony Motteux (1663–1718) was a translator and dramatist turned shopkeeper. In a letter to the *Spectator* No. 288 he describes the merchandise in his warehouse as china, tea, fans, Indian goods, and a great assortment of fabrics.

Page 44, line 34, paid: substituted by LM for "play'd." In bassette, "the *Pay* is when the *Punter* has won the *Couch* or first Stake . . . and being fearful . . . leaves off" (*Compleat Gamester* 179). Flavia's admirer was underwriting her next bet.

Page 46, line 44, Face: altered by LM to "Lines" in this MS, but she evidently preferred the original reading.

Page 46, line 46: LM substituted "Ressemblance" for "Remembrance," and "upraids" for "afflicts."

Page 48, line 71, Mirmillo: identified by Walpole as Sir Hans Sloane (1660–1753).

Page 48, line 75, Galen: perhaps Dr John Woodward (1665–1728), geologist and physician, who was called Galen by John Gay (*Poetry and Prose* I 293, II 615). Squirt was a character in *The Dispensary* (1699) by Samuel Garth (1661–1719).

Page 48, line 77: Machaon (identified by Walpole as Dr Garth) is the hero of *The Dispensary*. He was LM's family physician.

Page 49, last couplet on page: added by LM.

Page 49, Latin footnote: "The shepherds came too — All ask, 'whence is this love of thine?' Apollo came—and Sylvanus came with rustic glories on his brow—Pan came, Arcady's god, and we ourselves saw him crimsoned with vermilion and blood-red elderberries" (Virgil, x. 19–27 *passim*).

Page 52: The text printed here is a fair copy, most of it in LM's autograph, in Harrowby MSS, vol 256. Its title there is "Constantinople/To [name obliterated]." In the Arents MS, LM struck out "at Constantinople."

Page 52, line 1: The retirement theme, borrowed from Horace's Satires, II vi, was a popular one in Augustan English poetry.

Page 52, line 3: In the Arents MS, LM altered "clear" to "cool" and reduced "unto" to "to" and inserted "clear."

Page 52, line 17: In the winter of 1716 the Thames had been frozen solid.

Page 54, line 37: Lines 1 through 37 are in the hand of a scribe, the one who copied most of LM's Turkish Embassy Letters (Harrowby MSS vols 253, 254); the rest of the poem is in LM's hand.

Page 56, lines 52–55: These lines are not in the Arents MS; LM replaced them by lines 64–67.

Page 56, lines 62–63: In the Arents MS, these lines are put before the preceding couplet and then repeated.

Page 56, line 65: The Historical Pillar in the famous Hippodrome of Constantinople, LM wrote, had fallen down two years before (*Complete Letters* I 402).

Page 57: LM struck out lines 3 and 4, inserted a new couplet (not in the Harrowby MS), and then added the couplet just struck out (lines 46–47 in the Harrowby MS).

Page 58, line 68: Fanar or Phanar was the Greek quarter.

Page 58, lines 82–84: Voltaire quoted these lines (in a letter of Feb 1736) preceded by "I would not admire, as sais mylady Mary Wortley [the three lines of verse.] For how the devil should i admire a slave upon a horse?" (*Correspondence* et T. Besterman, Pléiade ed [1963–65] I 671). Since his quoted lines are closer to LM's (two) MS versions than to the 1720 printed text, he must have seen hers or a copy.

Page 60, line 93: In the Arents MS, LM altered "shining" to "gilded."

FIVE HUNDRED COPIES of this facsimile edition have been printed, on Mohawk Superfine paper, by The Meriden Gravure Company, Meriden, Connecticut. The type was set in the Printing Office of The New York Public Library, in Caslon Old Face, a faithful reproduction of the type cut by William Caslon, the great eighteenth-century English printer. Caslon modelled his designs on Dutch types of the late seventeenth century, but created a type extremely well suited to the groupings of English words. The italic swash characters in the display type were designed by the American artist Thomas Maitland Cleland in the early 1900's to be compatible with the original Caslon types, with its ligatures and other special characters in use in Caslon's day. The binding, with Holliston Roxite cloth and Strathmore Artlaid paper, and imitation Cockerell endpapers made by The Meriden Gravure Company, was done by the New Hampshire Bindery, Inc., Concord, New Hampshire.

Designed by Marilan Lund

This is copy number

293